Pinkalicious

CUPCAKE COOKBOOK

by Victoria Kann

recipe development by Patti Paige
photographs by Kristen Hess
cover photograph by Allen Owens

HARPER
An Imprint of HarperCollinsPublishers

Contents

Did you read the picture book *Pinkalicious* and imagine that you might eat too many cupcakes and turn pink? If you haven't read the picture book yet, don't worry, because this book will introduce you to the whole colorful world of *Pinkalicious*, *Purplicious*, *Silverlicious*, *Goldilicious*, and *Emeraldalicious* through cupcakes!

With designs and plans for more than twenty different projects—from a pinkalicious princess to a goldilicious unicorn—this book is bursting with imaginative and exciting ideas for cupcake decorating. In this introduction you'll find several basic recipes for cupcakes and frosting to get you started. Because the focus is on creativity and decorating, feel free to use store-bought mixes or recipes of your choice.

The Basics

Working with Color

The following pinkatastic recipes call for exact colors and brands to make the cupcakes in the photographs. Gel food coloring is recommended, because you can easily squeeze a drop at a time from the bottle to control how much color is added. Gel colors are more intense than the liquid food coloring from the grocery store. If you use the food coloring you have on hand or buy a brand other than the ones noted here, use the photographs as a guide as you mix and match your chosen brands and colors. The colors may turn out differently, but they'll still be lovely!

Natural food coloring will be less vibrant than colors from a bottle. Try beet juice, cranberry juice, or puréed strawberries or raspberries for pink, and puréed blueberries or blackberries or grape juice for purple.

Working with Cupcakes

All of the cupcakes in this book need a flat top to facilitate the frosting and decorating and sometimes for balancing one cupcake on top of another. When using a cupcake baked from a boxed cake mix, slice off the rounded top of the cupcake with a paring knife. Homemade-mix cupcakes usually bake up relatively flat and do not need to be cut.

Look for this symbol throughout the book for kid-friendly ideas!

Working with Quantities

If your cupcake decorating project calls for only a few cupcakes or cake pops, any extras will freeze beautifully. Wrap them in a layer of plastic wrap individually or together, then cover in tin foil. Frozen cupcakes or pops do not need to come to room temperature prior to decorating.

The special tips and techniques for Pinkalicious cupcake baking and decorating on the next seven pages are referred to in the instructions throughout the book. For Pinkalicious cupcake success, refer to this section often!

Pinkalicious Cupcake Recipes

I like to help assemble and measure all the ingredients before starting.

These recipes will work for all Pinkalicious cupcake decorating. Included below are pink, white, yellow, chocolate, and gluten-free versions. These moist cupcakes are sturdy and will hold up to handling and decorating.

Pink Cupcakes

A combination of strawberries and food coloring makes these pink. Feel free to omit the strawberries and use only the food coloring.

Makes 18 cupcakes or one 9 x 13-inch cake

- ♥ 3 cups unbleached all-purpose flour
- ♥ 1 tablespoon baking powder
- ♥ ¾ teaspoon salt
- ♥ 1 ½ cups sugar
- ♥ 6 tablespoons unsalted butter, softened
- ♥ ½ cup vegetable oil
- ♥ 1 tablespoon vanilla extract

- ♥ 5 large egg whites, at room temperature
- ♥ 1 cup whole milk
- ♥ 1 ½ cups finely chopped strawberries
- ♥ ¼ cup strawberry preserves
- ♥ a few drops of AmeriColor electric pink gel food coloring, optional

1 Preheat the oven to 350° and line one 12-cup cupcake pan and one 6-cup cupcake pan with paper liners.

2 Whisk the flour, baking powder, and salt together in a medium bowl and set aside. Place the sugar, butter, oil, and vanilla into a large mixing bowl (use the paddle attachment if using a stand mixer) and with the mixer on medium speed, beat the ingredients until fully incorporated and slightly fluffy, 3 to 5 minutes (the oil prevents the batter from getting super fluffy), scraping down the bowl with a rubber spatula, as needed.

3 Add the egg whites and beat until combined, about 1 minute. With the mixer on medium-low, add the flour mixture in three batches, alternating with the milk, and beginning and ending with the flour. Beat until the flour is only just incorporated. Drain the strawberries if necessary. Remove bowl from the mixer and fold in the strawberries. Stir in the strawberry preserves and squeeze in 1 to 5 drops of food coloring, if using. Scrape down the bowl until all traces of flour disappear and the strawberries and food coloring are well integrated into the batter, adding a drop or two more of color if you desire.

4 Fill each cupcake liner with 4 tablespoons of batter, place the pans in the oven, and bake for 12 to 14 minutes (rotating the pans halfway through the baking time) or until a toothpick inserted in the center of one of the cupcakes comes out clean. Let the pans cool on a wire rack until the cupcakes can be easily handled. Remove them from the pans and cool them on the wire rack until they reach room temperature.

White Cupcakes

Follow the pink cupcake recipe as written, but omit the strawberries and food coloring and fill the cupcake liners with 4 tablespoons of batter. When mixing the batter, leave it white or add any coloring, a drop at a time, to the mixing bowl to achieve the specific shade needed. These are ideal as a base for any color.

Yellow Cupcakes

Makes 18 cupcakes or one 9 x 13-inch cake

- 3 cups unbleached all-purpose flour
- 1 tablespoon baking powder
- ¾ teaspoon salt
- 1 ½ cups sugar
- 6 tablespoons unsalted butter, softened

- ½ cup vegetable oil
- 1 tablespoon vanilla extract
- 5 large egg yolks, at room temperature
- 1 cup whole milk

1 Preheat the oven to 350° and line one 12-cup cupcake pan and one 6-cup cupcake pan with paper liners.

2 Whisk the flour, baking powder, and salt together in a medium bowl and set aside. Place the sugar, butter, oil, and vanilla into a large mixing bowl (use the paddle attachment if using a stand mixer), and with the mixer on medium speed, beat the ingredients until fully incorporated and slightly fluffy, 4 to 6 minutes for a stand mixer and 7 to 8 minutes using a hand mixer (the oil will prevent the batter from getting super fluffy), scraping down the bowl with a rubber spatula as needed.

3 Add the egg yolks one at a time and beat until combined. With the mixer on medium-low, add the flour mixture in three batches, alternating with the milk, and beginning and ending with the flour. Beat until the flour is only just incorporated. Scrape down the bowl until all traces of flour disappear.

4 Fill each cupcake liner with 4 tablespoons of batter, place the pans in the oven, and bake them for 12 to 14 minutes (rotating the pans halfway through the baking time) or until a toothpick inserted in the center of one of the cupcakes comes out clean. Let the pans cool on a wire rack until the cupcakes can be easily handled. Remove them from the pans and cool them on the wire rack until they reach room temperature.

Chocolate Cupcakes

Makes 18 cupcakes or one 9 x 13-inch cake

- 2 ¼ cups unbleached all-purpose flour
- 1 tablespoon baking powder
- ¾ teaspoon salt
- ¾ cup Dutch-process cocoa powder
- 1 cup boiling water
- 1 cup sugar
- ½ cup packed dark brown sugar
- 6 tablespoons unsalted butter, softened
- ½ cup vegetable oil
- 1 tablespoon vanilla extract
- 5 large egg yolks, at room temperature

1 Preheat the oven to 350° and line one 12-cup cupcake pan and one 6-cup cupcake pan with paper liners.

2 Whisk the flour, baking powder, and salt together in a medium bowl and set aside. Combine the cocoa powder and the boiling water and whisk until well incorporated ensuring there are no lumps of cocoa powder. Set aside. Place the sugars, butter, oil, and vanilla into a large mixing bowl (use the paddle attachment if using a stand mixer), and with the mixer on medium speed, beat the ingredients until fully incorporated and slightly fluffy, 4 to 6 minutes for a stand mixer and 7 to 8 minutes using a hand mixer (the oil will prevent the batter from getting super fluffy), scraping down the bowl with a rubber spatula as needed.

3 Add the egg yolks and beat until combined. With the mixer on medium-low, add the flour mixture in three batches, alternating with the cocoa mixture, and beginning and ending with the flour. Beat until the flour is only just incorporated. Scrape down the bowl until all traces of flour disappear.

4 Fill each cupcake liner with 4 tablespoons of batter, place the pans in the oven, and bake for 12 to 14 minutes (rotating the pans halfway through the baking time) or until a toothpick inserted in the center of one of the cupcakes comes out clean. Let the pans cool on a wire rack until the cupcakes can be easily handled. Remove them from the pans and cool them on the wire racks until they reach room temperature.

I like to mix in a large bowl so nothing goes over the edge!

Gluten-Free Yellow Cupcakes

The flour in these recipes is a widely available store-bought blend from Bob's Red Mill or King Arthur. If you would rather make your own gluten-free flour for this yellow cupcake, simply whisk together 1 ½ cups superfine brown or white rice flour, ¾ cup tapioca flour, and ¾ cup potato starch in a medium bowl and substitute this mixture for the Bob's Red Mill or King Arthur blend.

Makes 24 cupcakes or one 9 x 13-inch cake

- 3 cups Bob's Red Mill or King Arthur Gluten-Free all-purpose baking flour.
- 1 ½ teaspoons xanthan gum
- 1 tablespoon baking powder
- ¾ teaspoon salt
- 1 ½ cups sugar

- 6 tablespoons unsalted butter, softened
- ½ cup vegetable oil
- 1 tablespoon vanilla extract
- 5 large egg yolks, at room temperature
- 1 cup whole milk

1 Preheat the oven to 350° and line two 12-cup cupcake pans with paper liners.

2 Whisk the flour, xanthan gum, baking powder, and salt in a medium bowl and set aside. Place the sugar, butter, oil, and vanilla into a large mixing bowl (use the paddle attachment if using a stand mixer), and with the mixer on medium speed, beat the ingredients until fully incorporated and slightly fluffy, 4 to 6 minutes for a stand mixer and 7 to 8 minutes using a hand mixer (the oil will prevent the batter from getting super fluffy), scraping down the bowl with a rubber spatula as needed.

3 Add the egg yolks and beat until combined. With the mixer on medium-low, add the flour mixture in three batches, alternating with the milk, and beginning and ending with the flour. Beat until the flour is only just incorporated. Scrape down the bowl until all traces of flour disappear.

4 Fill each cupcake liner with 4 tablespoons of batter, place the pans in the oven, and bake for 12 to 14 minutes (rotating the pans halfway through the baking time) or until a toothpick inserted in the center of one of the cupcakes comes out clean. Let the pans cool on a wire rack until the cupcakes can be easily handled. Remove them from the pans and cool them on the wire rack until they reach room temperature.

Gluten-Free Chocolate Cupcakes

The flour in this recipe is a widely available store-bought blend from Bob's Red Mill or King Arthur. If you would rather make your own for these chocolate cupcakes, just whisk together 1 cup, 2 tablespoons superfine brown or white rice flour; ½ cup, 1 tablespoon tapioca flour; and ½ cup, 1 tablespoon potato starch in a medium bowl and substitute this for the Bob's Red Mill or King Arthur. *Please note that this substitute mix is different from the one for the Gluten-Free Yellow Cupcakes.*

Makes 24 cupcakes or one 9 x 13-inch cake

- 2 ¼ cups Bob's Red Mill or King Arthur Gluten-Free all-purpose baking flour
- 1 ½ teaspoons xanthan gum
- 1 tablespoon baking powder
- ¾ teaspoon salt
- ¾ cup Dutch-process cocoa powder
- 1 cup boiling water

- 1 cup sugar
- ½ cup packed dark brown sugar
- 6 tablespoons unsalted butter, softened
- ½ cup vegetable oil
- 1 tablespoon vanilla extract
- 5 large egg yolks, at room temperature

1 Preheat the oven to 350° and line two 12-cup cupcake pans with paper liners.

2 Whisk the flour, xanthan gum, baking powder, and salt in a medium bowl and set aside. Combine the cocoa powder and the boiling water and whisk until well incorporated. Set aside. Place the sugars, butter, oil, and vanilla into a large mixing bowl (use the paddle attachment if using a stand mixer) and with the mixer on medium speed, beat the ingredients until fully incorporated and slightly fluffy, 3 to 5 minutes (the oil will prevent the batter from getting super fluffy), scraping down the bowl with a rubber spatula as needed.

3 Add the egg yolks and beat until combined. With the mixer on medium-low, add the flour mixture in three batches, alternating with the cocoa mixture, and beginning and ending with the flour. Beat until the flour is only just incorporated. Scrape down the bowl until all traces of flour disappear.

4 Fill each cupcake liner with 4 tablespoons of batter, place the pans in the oven, and bake for 14 to 16 minutes (rotating the pans halfway through the baking time) or until a toothpick inserted in the center of one of the cupcakes comes out clean. Let the pans cool on a wire rack until the cupcakes can be easily handled. Remove them from the pans and cool them on the wire rack until they reach room temperature.

Frosting and Icing

Pinkalicious cupcakes can be decorated with store-bought or homemade frosting. While the store-bought frosting can be easier to use because it holds its shape well, homemade frosting tastes better. It's your choice!

Buttercream Frosting
Makes about 6 cups

- 1 cup shortening
- ¾ cup butter, softened
- 8 cups confectioners' sugar, sifted
- ½ teaspoon salt
- ½ cup whole milk
- 1 tablespoon vanilla

Combine shortening and butter in a large mixing bowl and beat on medium speed until fully incorporated. Reduce mixer speed to medium low, slowly add half the sugar and salt, and mix until well blended. Add milk and vanilla and, slowly, the rest of the sugar. When all sugar is incorporated, increase speed to medium-high and beat until thick and spreadable, 5 to 7 minutes. Use immediately or store, tightly covered, at room temperature for up to 3 days. Rewhip before using.

Spreading
When spreading, always dip your utensil—a small offset spatula or butter knife—into warm water first.

Place a dollop of frosting on the cupcake. Holding the cupcake in one hand, gently spread frosting around the top of the cupcake with utensil, rotating as you do so. Do not get frosting on the liner or go past the edge of the cupcake. To remove excess, wipe off your spreading utensil and make a clean swipe around the cupcake.

For a cupcake with a generous dome of frosting, scoop more frosting onto your cupcake and use your utensil to shape it into a dome with smooth, long strokes.

Melting
Homemade frosting cannot be melted. If your recipe calls for melted frosting, you must use store-bought.

Place frosting in a microwave-safe bowl and microwave for 5 to 10 seconds. Stir gently with spoon. Frosting should be consistency of lightly whipped cream. If it is too thick, microwave it for 5 seconds more.

Royal Icing
Makes about 4 cups

- ¼ cup meringue powder (available in specialty baking stores or online)
- 4 cups confectioners' sugar, sifted
- ½ cup warm water

Combine meringue powder and confectioners' sugar in a large mixing bowl. Beat on medium until thoroughly combined. Slowly add water and beat for 7 to 10 minutes, until icing is glossy, fluffy, and thick. Use immediately or keep in airtight container for up to 3 days.

Using Color with Frosting
While the mixer is running, add food coloring, a drop at a time, to the frosting in the bowl until desired color is reached. Gel and paste provide the most vibrant colors, but liquid coloring from the grocery store will work in a pinch.

Decorations

Place small decorations precisely with tweezers; use fingers for others.

Depending on texture and shape of candy, use either scissors or a small, sharp paring knife to cut. Use scissors for cutting candy flattened into a sheet or a strip. Use a paring knife to cut and score sprinkles or wafers.

Gumdrops and other sticky candies can be rolled into flat pieces and cut into different shapes. Roll these out on a nonstick surface sprinkled with sparkling sugar to prevent them from sticking.

To attach candies and edible decorations to cupcakes, use piped frosting, royal icing, or candy melts. All three are excellent edible "glues." Candy melts provide the strongest hold, while royal icing is the least visible.

Candy Melts

These small wafers can be melted and used to coat cake pops or cupcakes. Available in baking specialty shops, craft shops, and online. See Sources.

Piping and Gluing

Fill a Ziploc bag with candy melts. Place the unsealed bag in the microwave and microwave on high for about 10 to 15 seconds. Remove bag from the microwave and carefully massage melts to soften. Return bag to microwave and repeat process until contents are completely melted. Press out excess air and seal bag. Cut a tiny hole in the corner of bag.

Dipping

Place candy melts in a small, microwave-safe bowl and microwave on high for 30 seconds. Remove melts from the microwave and stir with a wooden spoon. If they are not completely melted, return them to the microwave for another 15 seconds, until smooth.

Piping and Gluing with Buttercream Frosting and Royal Icing

Piped frosting and icing can be used as glue for attaching candies, or as decoration in its own right.

Fill a Ziploc bag with frosting or icing. Press out excess air and seal. Move the frosting or icing to one corner of the bag and cut a tiny hole in that corner. When piping, hold the bag with two hands, squeezing the bag gently and evenly with one hand while holding the tip of the bag steady with the other hand.

Sprinkles, Dust, Sugars, and Pearls

Confetti sprinkles (small, round, and flat), nonpareils (tiny and spherical), sprinkles (tiny sticks, known as jimmies in New England), and heart- and star-shaped sprinkles add color and texture. Disco dust and pearl luster dust create shimmer and sparkle when applied over frosting or rice paper. Sanding sugar (very finely ground sugar) and sparkling sugar (larger sugar crystals that also come in handy when rolling out sticky gumdrops) are both sweet and glittery.

Candy pearls and dragées are little round balls, larger than nonpareils, for finishing touches and accents. However, some people prefer not to consume dragées—at least not too many! They are not sold in California, so feel free to substitute candy pearls or other small, ball-shaped candies instead.

I like to be creativealicious with the decorations!

11

Pinkalicious Party

This pretty pink cupcake with a cherry on top is the essential Pinkalicious cupcake.
Whip up a batch and then make one as big as a cake!

Classic

Makes 12

- ♡ 24 pink cupcakes, from a boxed cake mix or homemade, 12 with pink liners, 12 with any color
- ♡ 12 cups frosting, store-bought or homemade, tinted with a drop or two of electric pink AmeriColor Soft Gel Paste Food Coloring (creating a light pink color)
- ♡ 1 cup frosting, store-bought or homemade, tinted with several drops of electric pink AmeriColor Soft Gel Paste Food Coloring (creating a dark pink color)
- ♡ Wilton nonpareils, white
- ♡ 12 Maraschino cherries

I save the leftover cake and cupcake scraps to make teeny tiny cupcakes. (see p. 16)

1 Cut off the tops of all 24 cupcakes so they are flat. Remove the liners from 12 cupcakes. Turn those 12 cupcakes upside down and use light pink frosting to glue them to the tops of the 12 cupcakes in pink liners. Refrigerate 20 minutes until very firm.

2 With a sharp paring knife carve the top cupcakes into a dome shape. Cover the domes with a thin layer of frosting. Refrigerate 15 minutes until firm.

3 Generously frost the domes with more light pink frosting. While the frosting is still soft, place the non-pareils in a bowl, and dip just the top of the dome into the nonpareils.

4 Fill a pastry bag fitted with a #18 star tip with the dark pink frosting, and pipe a scalloped swirl border around the edge of each cupcake. Place a cherry on top of each cupcake.

Huge

This pinkatastic wonder is really a layer cake!

- ♡ Four 7-inch pink cake layers, from two boxed cake mixes or homemade
- ♡ 6 cups frosting, store-bought or homemade, tinted with a drop or two of electric pink AmeriColor Soft Gel Paste Food Coloring (creating a light pink color)
- ♡ 2 cups frosting, store-bought or homemade, tinted with several drops of electric pink AmeriColor Soft Gel Paste Food Coloring (creating a dark pink color)
- ♡ Fondarific sculpting chocolate, white
- ♡ AmeriColor Soft Gel Paste Food Coloring, red
- ♡ 1 piece red string licorice or Gustaf's strawberry laces
- ♡ Wilton sugar pearls, white

1 Make 2 two-layer cakes. Put frosting between the two layers in each cake. Refrigerate both cakes 15 minutes until firm.

2 Transfer one of the layer cakes to a 6-inch cardboard cake round, and with a knife taper the sides to the shape of a cupcake base. The top should be 7 inches in diameter and the bottom should be about 5 inches in diameter. The base shape should be about 3 ½ inches tall. Set the cake scraps aside. Frost with a thin layer of dark pink frosting and refrigerate 15 minutes until firm.

3 Once firm, remove both cakes from refrigerator and use light pink frosting to glue one cake on top of the other. Refrigerate again to firm. Carve the edges off the top two-layer cake to rough out a dome shape. In a separate bowl, mix together enough light pink frosting and cake scraps to make a cake pop mixture. Next, use the cake pop mixture to finish molding a perfectly rounded dome. Use your hands to pat and smooth this mixture on top, making the dome about 4 inches high. This dome should be slightly larger in proportion to the cupcake base.

4 Cover the dome in a thin layer of light pink frosting and refrigerate 15 minutes until firm. Frost the bottom with dark pink frosting and the top of the dome again with light pink until the frosting is smooth.

5 To Make a Cherry: Tint a 1-inch round ball of the sculpting chocolate red. Cut a 2 ½-inch piece of licorice and insert it into the red chocolate ball to make the stem.

When I want just one more, this is the cupcake I want!

6 Fill a pastry bag fitted with a #22 star tip with the dark pink frosting and pipe the scalloped swirl border. Replace the star tip with a #12 tip, or prepare a Ziploc bag (see Decorations, p. 11) with the frosting and pipe vertical lines on the base to make it look like a cupcake wrapper!

7 Place the cherry in the center of the dome and place the pearls around the top of the dome.

Teeny Tiny Pinky Cupcake

This itty-bitty, thimble-sized cupcake is really made of yummy cake pop.

Makes 12

♡ 1 cup frosting
♡ 1 cup of cake scraps
♡ ½ cup Wilton candy melts, dark pink
♡ Styrofoam block
♡ 1 cup frosting, store-bought or homemade, tinted with a drop or two of electric pink AmeriColor Soft Gel Paste Food Coloring (creating a light pink color)

♡ ½ cup royal icing, tinted with several drops of electric pink AmeriColor Soft Gel Paste Food Coloring (creating a dark pink color)
♡ 5 Sweet's jumbo gumdrops, red
♡ ¼ cup store-bought frosting, tinted with red AmeriColor Soft Gel Paste Food Coloring

1 Mix cake scraps saved from another recipe with one cup of frosting (see Cake Pop Garden, p. 22). Freeze the cake pop mixture for 15 minutes. Remove it from the freezer and, using a paring knife, cut out 12 small cupcake-shaped pieces, about ½ inch each. Freeze for 10 minutes more.

2 Prepare a bowl of the melted candy melts (see Decorations, p.11). One at a time, stick a toothpick in a small frozen cupcake. Hold the toothpick and completely immerse the cupcake in the bowl of melts. Remove, let the excess drip off, and stick the cupcake into a Styrofoam block. Repeat with all 12 cupcakes. Set aside to dry.

3 Prepare a Ziploc bag with light pink frosting (see Decorations, p. 11) and pipe a smooth dome of frosting on each cupcake.

4 Fill a pastry bag fitted with a #00 tip with the royal icing, or use a Ziploc bag (see Decorations, p. 11). Pipe the vertical lines on the cake part of the cupcake for the liner and the scalloped border around the edge of the frosting dome on each.

5 Cut off 12 small pieces of gumdrop and roll them between your fingers to make 12 cherries.

6 Melt the red frosting (see Frosting and Icing, p.10). Using a spoon, dip the cherries into the melted icing, one at a time, until completely covered. Let dry. Place a cherry on each cupcake, gluing with a dot of royal icing if needed.

Mommy says
"You get what you get, and you don't get upset!"

Purple Power Tower

Purple has never been yummier than in this tower of purplicious cupcakes!

Makes 12 cupcakes

- 12 white cupcakes, from a boxed cake mix or homemade, white liners
- 8 cups frosting, white, store-bought or homemade
- AmeriColor Soft Gel Paste Food Coloring, electric pink
- AmeriColor Soft Gel Paste Food Coloring, electric purple
- CK sanding sugar, purple
- Wilton sugar pearls, blue
- Wilton sugar pearls, white
- Wilton jumbo nonpareils, purple
- Wilton jumbo nonpareils, white
- CK sixlets, purple
- CK sprinkles, purple
- 10 Necco wafers, white
- Wilton Jumbo Heart Sprinkles, pink
- Wilton jumbo confetti sprinkles, lavender
- 3 pastry tips, #s 16, 21, and 30

1 To Ice the Cupcakes: Divide the icing into four bowls. Tint one with pink food coloring, the other three with different amounts of both purple and pink coloring for light, medium, or dark purple. The lightest will need one or two drops of each color; the darkest, three or more. Ice the cupcakes: Three in dark purple, building the icing to a dome shape; three in pink with a dome shape; four in medium purple with a dome shape; one in dark purple with a flat top, one in pink with a flat top. Use the remaining icing to fill pastry bags, fitted with three different tips (#16, #21, and #30), or Ziploc bags, as needed.

2 To Decorate the Cupcakes:

Spiky piped stars: To make spiky stars, touch the tip of a pastry bag to an iced cupcake, pulling back while squeezing and releasing the pressure to finish. Use dark frosting with the #21 tip and medium purple icing with the #30 tip to cover the top with stars. Use the smallest tip, #16, to pipe smaller stars in a lighter color between the others. Alternately, pipe rows of spiky stars in different shades. **Tricolor rings:** Use separate bags of pink, medium purple, and dark purple icing fitted with #21 tip. Squeeze concentric rings, one of each color, and top with a round candy. **Rosette swirls:** Fill a pastry bag fitted with a #30 tip with medium purple icing. Start at the top and work down, touching the tip to an iced cupcake and making a swirling motion while squeezing to form rosettes, releasing the pressure to finish. Place white sugar pearls between the rosettes. **Dotted tops:** Decorate an iced cupcake with a pattern of evenly spaced sugar pearls, white jumbo nonpareils, or jumbo confetti. Use contrasting or complementary colors. **Decorated edges:** Roll the edge in sprinkles or sanding sugar. **Grids and spirals:** Fill a Ziploc bag with dark purple icing (see Decorations, p. 11) and pipe a grid. Fill the grid with purple sixlets and sugar pearls. Or pipe a long spiral over the dome, beginning at the top center of the cupcake and finishing at the edge. Top with a sugar pearl. **Flower petal edge:** Cut white Necco wafers in half and attach to the edge with icing, around the entire cupcake. Place jumbo purple nonpareils in between each petal, at its base. Place a round purple candy in the center of the cupcake half and attach to the edge with icing. Place jumbo purple nonpareils in between each petal at its base. Place a round purple candy in the center of the cupcake.

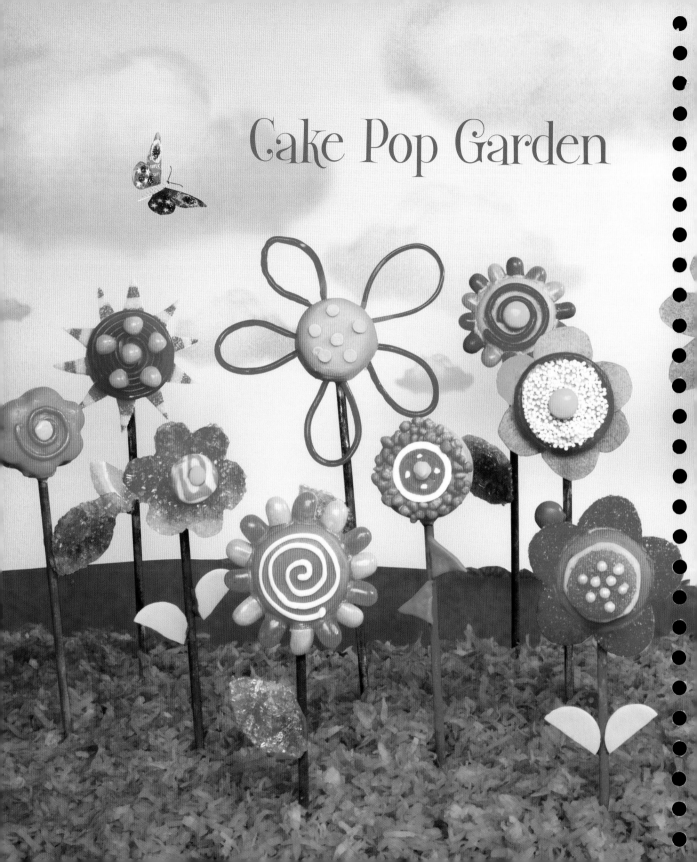

Cake Pop Garden

Cake Pop Garden

1 To Make Cake Pops:

- One 13 x 9-inch baked cake, from a boxed cake mix or homemade
- 2 cups frosting, store-bought or homemade
- 2 cups Wilton candy melts, light pink
- 2 cups Wilton candy melts, dark pink
- 24 8-inch green lollipop sticks

Crumble the cake into a large bowl. Add frosting and combine thoroughly. Transfer mixture to a 13 x 9-inch baking pan and flatten. Cover with plastic wrap and freeze, 15 minutes.

With 1 ½-inch flower- and circle-shaped cookie cutters, cut shapes from half of the frozen cake and frosting mixture. Roll ¾-inch and 1½-inch balls from the remaining half. Set the shapes and balls on a parchment-lined cookie sheet, cover with plastic wrap and freeze for an additional 15 minutes.

Cut one side of some balls to make a flat "face"; leave the rest round. Prepare two bowls of candy melts, one of light pink, one of dark pink (Decorations, p. 11). Dip the ends of green 8-inch lollipop sticks into the light pink or dark pink melts and insert one into the base of each flower pop. Freeze again for 15 minutes.

Holding them by their sticks, immerse each cake pop in the melts. Tap gently to remove any excess. Cover half of the pops in one color and half in the other. Insert sticks into a block of Styrofoam, allowing melts to dry and set.

2 To Make Flowers: Start with petals, then stigma (the center), and then the leaves.

- 12 cake pops, in a variety of shapes, dipped in light and dark pink candy melts
- 1 cup Wilton candy melts, light pink
- 1 cup Wilton candy melts, dark pink
- rice paper
- Wilton pearl dust, orchid pink, lilac purple
- Gustaf's strawberry laces
- AirHeads Xtremes Lemonade Sour Belts,
- Boston Fruit Slice, yellow, red
- Sweet's jumbo gumdrops, red, orange, green, yellow, white
- Wilton sparkling sugar, white, pink
- Jelly Belly jelly bean, pink
- Jelly Belly licorice pastels, pink
- Necco wafers, green, pink, white
- Now and Later soft taffy, pink, yellow
- Smooth & Melty Nonpareil Mint Chocolate Chips, yellow, pink
- Wilton nonpareils, white
- 2 teaspoons Wilton meringue powder
- M&M's, pink, pastel green, yellow
- Wonka Nerds, strawberry
- Wilton FoodWriter, extra fine tip, orange
- Trolli Peachie O's
- Betty Crocker Fruit Roll-Ups, strawberry
- Haribo Wheels, strawberry
- Wilton Mini Confetti Sprinkles, yellow, white
- Wilton Mini Flower Sprinkles, yellow
- Wilton sugar pearls, yellow
- Rip Rolls, green apple
- 1 cup Wilton candy melts, green

Petals: TULIP OR DAISY Rub pearl dust on rice paper before cutting out petals. For tulip, use two pieces of rice paper, rub a different pearl dust on each one, and cut a small tulip from one piece of rice paper and a large tulip from the other. Glue the small to the large with candy melts (Decorations, p. 11) and then glue the entire tulip to the flat side of a cake pop ball. LICORICE OR AIRHEAD LOOP PETALS Use a toothpick to make holes around the perimeter of a pop. Cut licorice into five 4-inch lengths. Cut apart pink and red stripes from Air-Heads and cut strips into seven 1½-inch lengths. Pipe candy melt into each hole. Loop the candy and insert the ends in the holes. AIRHEAD TRIANGLES OR BOSTON FRUIT SLICES PETALS Cut candy into the desired shape and glue around the pop with candy melts. Roll out gumdrops to ¼ inch on a nonstick surface sprinkled with sparkling sugar, and then cut flattened gumdrops into a flower shape. Glue gumdrop shape to the flat side of a cake pop ball with candy melts. OTHER PETALS Cut off a bit of several jelly beans and licorice pastels and glue the cut sides to the perimeter of the pop. WINDMILL PETALS Score and cut pink Necco wafers into quarters. Glue to the perimeter of the pop with candy melts.

First I wash my hands and then I mush the scraps and frosting together.

Stigmas (centers): SWIRLS Roll taffy into a thin strand between your fingers and glue to the cake pop in a swirl shape using candy melts. BALLS Roll taffy into a small ball and glue it to the center of a pop. COMBO Combine a swirl and ball together on one pop. LAYERS Shave off the pointy side of a Smooth & Melty nonpareil so that it lies flat and glue it with candy melts to the center of the flower, with the uncut side facing up. Then cut a circle from a Boston Fruit Slice and glue it, using candy melts, to the center of the nonpareil. Combine the meringue powder with two tablespoons of water and brush the mixture onto the Smooth & Melty. Sprinkle small white nonpareils on top. PEACHIE O'S Cut off the outer layer of a Gummy Ring in the shape of a circle. Glue a pink M&M in the middle of the cut-out Gummy with candy melts, then glue the combined M&M-Gummy onto the flat side of a cake pop flower. FRUIT ROLL-UP From a Fruit Roll-Up, cut a circle that is slightly larger than a Smooth & Melty nonpareil. Shave off the pointy tip of the Smooth & Melty and glue it, uncut side up, with candy melts to the Fruit Roll-Up circle. Glue the stigma to the center of a pop. NECCO WAFERS Using the orange edible marker, draw a button on a white Necco Wafer. Pipe candy melts on the back of the wafer, and attach to the flat side of a cake pop. Pipe additional candy melts along the edge of the pop and around the wafer. Sprinkle Nerds on the candy melts and press them into position. Roll yellow taffy into a tiny ball and glue it to the center of the button. LICORICE AND JELLY BEAN VARIATIONS Glue a licorice wheel to the flat side of a cake pop. Cut jelly beans in half and glue the halves onto the licorice wheel with candy melts.

Leaves: Prepare a bag of green candy melts (Decorations, p. 11). Set aside.

MARBLED LEAVES Press together red (or orange), green, and yellow gumdrops. Roll out the multicolored gumdrop lump to ¼ inch thick on a nonstick surface sprinkled with sparkling sugar. Cut out the leaf shapes. Pipe a dot or two of green candy melts onto the stick of a pop, and hold the leaves in place until set. GREEN LEAVES Cut pastel green M&Ms, Boston Fruit Slices, or Rip Rolls into leaf shapes, or score and cut Necco wafers in half. Attach to a stick with candy melts and hold until set.

Princess Pinkalicious

Make Princess Pinkalicious, her imaginary
unicorn, Goldilicious, and a pink castle! Filling goodie bags?
What could be more joyful than Pinkalicious's star wand?
It's a frosted sugar cookie covered with disco dust—
a perfect party favor!

Princess Pinkalicious

- 2 white cupcakes, from a boxed cake mix or homemade, one with a pink liner
- ½ cup frosting, store-bought or homemade, tinted with copper flesh-tone AmeriColor Soft Gel Paste Food Coloring
- ½ cup frosting, store-bought or homemade, tinted with electric pink AmeriColor Soft Gel Paste Food Coloring
- ½ cup Wilton candy melts, brown
- 1 Starburst, pink
- 1 AirHeads taffy, red
- 1 Laffy Taffy, pink
- Wilton sparkling sugar, white
- 1 square graham cracker, 2-inch x 2-inch

If you use a Ziploc of candy melts to make Pinkalicious's features, make the hole in the bag super tiny for best results.

1 To Make the Base: Peel the wrapper off the cupcake without the pink liner. Start ½ inch from the top of the cupcake and slice off a corner of the side at a 45-degree angle to make a flat oval shape. The angle should not be sharp; the top of the cupcake will be the face and the cut oval will connect to the base cupcake. Spread a thin layer of the flesh-tone frosting smoothly on the face.

Spread a generous layer of the electric pink frosting onto the top of the cupcake in the pink liner. Press the flat, oval, cut side of the face cupcake into the pink frosting. Freeze until firm, about 10 to 15 minutes.

2 To Make the Face, Hat, and Hair: Prepare a Ziploc bag of melted candy melts (Decorations, p. 11). Trace the template for Pinkalicious's pigtails (p. 63) on parchment paper with a black permanent marker. Place another piece of parchment paper over it and put both on a cookie sheet. Using the bag of candy melts, trace the template for the pigtails and fill it in. Refrigerate until hard.

Remove the cupcakes from the freezer and pipe Pinkalicious's bangs, eyes, nose, and eyebrows onto the "face" cupcake.

With a rolling pin, roll out the Starburst, AirHead, and Laffy Taffy candies to ⅛-inch thick on a nonstick surface sprinkled with white sparkling sugar to prevent stickiness.

Trace the template for Pinkalicious's hat (p. 63) on parchment paper, cut it out, and use it to cut hat shapes from the graham cracker and the AirHeads; also roll a small piece of AirHeads into a half moon for her mouth. Cut two small discs from the Starburst for the cheeks and a thin strip of Laffy Taffy for the hat ribbon. Place the cheeks and mouth onto the cupcake.

Peel the candy melt pigtails off the parchment paper with a thin spatula. Poke a hole on either side of the face, squeeze some candy melts into each hole, and carefully insert a pigtail into each.

With candy melts, glue the AirHeads triangle on the triangle-shaped graham cracker and the Laffy Taffy ribbon to the tip of the hat. To make the hat sparkle more, first dip the AirHeads-covered graham cracker into white sanding sugar.

Pipe candy melts on the top edge of the face to make her bangs then press the bottom edge of the graham cracker hat into the cupcake, piping more candy melts behind the hat to ensure it is securely fastened.

Refrigerate the cupcake until all candy melts harden completely.

Star Wand

Makes 12 wands

- 12 long wooden skewers or dowels
- AmeriColor Soft Gel Paste Food Coloring, electric pink
- One 16.5-ounce package of store-bought sugar cookie dough
- ½ cup all-purpose flour, plus more for dusting the work surface
- ½ cup royal icing, tinted with electric yellow AmeriColor Soft Gel Paste Food Coloring
- AmeriColor Soft Gel Paste Food Coloring, gold
- 2 teaspoons Wilton meringue powder
- CK disco dust, baby green
- Twelve 12-inch ribbons, pink

I can paint the sticks Pinkalicious pink!

1 To Make the Wand: Preheat the oven to 350° and line two cookie sheets with parchment paper.

Paint the 12 sticks pink with the electric pink food coloring. Let dry.

In a medium bowl, combine the sugar cookie dough with the flour, kneading the flour completely into the dough. Roll the dough out to ¼-inch thick on a nonstick surface dusted with flour. Trace the star template (p. 63) onto a piece of cardboard with a black permanent marker and cut it out; use it to cut stars from the rolled-out dough.

Insert the sticks into the sides of the stars. Roll gently on the stick to ease it into the cookie at least halfway. Do not break the surface of the cookie.

Bake following manufacturer's directions, remove to a wire rack, and let cool.

2 To Decorate the Stars: Place half of the royal icing in a pastry bag fitted with a #1 tip, or fill a Ziploc bag (Decorations, p. 11). Pipe around the edge of the star, as close to the edge as possible. Let set. Flood or thin the rest of the royal icing with water, a teaspoon at a time, to the consistency of paint.

Paint the icing on the cookies, up to the piped edge but not over it. Let set.

Thin some gold food coloring with half a teaspoon of water, mixing more coloring and/or water to get a light brown color. Lightly brush the edges of the star with the light brown food coloring for shading.

Combine the meringue powder and 2 tablespoons of water. Using a pastry brush, brush all over the iced cookie, and blend the brown food color into the yellow. While still wet, sprinkle disco dust on top of the star. Let dry.

Tie the ribbons around the sticks right below the stars, and cut the ends of the ribbons into V shapes.

Goldilicious

Makes one Goldilicious

- 1 batch Rice Krispies Treats, at room temperature
- 2 cups white frosting, store-bought
- 1 white cupcake, from a boxed cake mix or homemade, in a gold liner
- 1 Stretch Island Fruit Co. All-Natural Fruit Strip, Mango Sunrise
- 1 mini marshmallow

- ½ cup frosting, store-bought or homemade, tinted with electric yellow AmeriColor Soft Gel Paste Food Coloring
- 2 DecoPac edible confetti sprinkles, blue
- 2 Wilton jumbo confetti sprinkles, pink
- 1 Tootsie Roll
- ¼ cup frosting, store-bought or homemade, tinted gray using one drop of black AmeriColor Soft Gel Paste Food Coloring
- Wilton Flowerful Medley 6-Mix Sprinkle Assortment, 15 green flowers, 10 pink flowers

I like to roll the Rice Krispies Treats into balls.

1 To Make Goldilicious: Roll three balls from a piece of Rice Krispies Treat: one as big as a Ping-Pong ball, for Goldilicious's head (about .50 ounce), one a little smaller than a Ping-Pong ball, for Goldilicious's nose (about .35 ounce), and one slightly larger than a Ping-Pong ball, for Goldilicious's neck (about .65 ounce).

Press the smallest ball into the medium ball to make the head and nose, ensuring they are tightly bonded. Place this shape on the largest ball, and press and mold this ball to make the neck. The neck should have a flat bottom and should be slightly smaller in diameter than the top of the cupcake. The finished shape should be 3 to 4 inches tall. If parts start to separate, press additional small pieces of Rice Krispies Treats onto the seams.

Generously spread the white frosting onto the cupcake, giving it some height. Glue the head to the cupcake by pressing it into the frosting. Spread additional frosting around the edge of the cupcake and up around the base of the neck. Freeze until set.

Melt 1 cup of white frosting (Frosting and Icing, p. 10). Remove the shape from the freezer and, holding it upside down, dunk it into the bowl of melted frosting.

Pull out, let drip upside down briefly, then turn right side up and smooth any drips. Freeze again for 5 minutes. Remelt the leftover frosting in the microwave, remove Goldilicious from the freezer, and dunk a second time in the melted frosting. Let drip upside down again briefly, and then smooth again. Freeze until hardened.

2 To Make the Face and Mane: Cut the fruit strip in half and roll one half into a skinny cone shape for the horn, about 1 ½ to 2 inches long. Trim as necessary.

Prepare a Ziploc bag with the unmelted white frosting (Decorations, p. 11) and use it to glue the horn on. Snip the mini marshmallow in half and glue each half onto the head with white frosting for ears. Prepare a Ziploc bag with the yellow frosting (Decorations, p. 11). Pipe Goldilicious's curly yellow mane. Place the blue confetti sprinkle eyes and pink Jumbo confetti sprinkle cheeks. Roll a small piece of Tootsie Roll, cut it, and position it for the mouth. Prepare a Ziploc bag with the gray frosting (Decorations, p. 11) and pipe dots for her nostrils.

Position the green flower sprinkles to create the wreath, and glue on a few pink flowers with the white frosting.

Pinkalicious Castle

Makes one castle

- 1 white cupcake, in a dark pink liner, from a boxed cake mix or homemade
- 1 white jumbo cupcake, in a dark pink liner, from a boxed cake mix or homemade
- 1 cup frosting, store-bought or homemade, tinted with electric pink AmeriColor Soft Gel Paste Food Coloring
- 1 cup Wilton candy melts, pink
- 1 sugar cone
- ½ cup India Tree sparkling sugar, bright white
- CK disco dust, baby green
- 1 Rold Gold pretzel ptick
- 1 CK candy bead pearl, hot pink
- 4 sticks Freedent spearmint gum
- 5 Hi-Chew fruit chews, strawberry
- 2 drageés, pink

1 To Make the Tower: Generously spread the pink frosting on the cupcakes, giving them some height. Stack the smaller cupcake on top of the larger and press together. Refrigerate.

Prepare a bowl of melted candy melts (Frosting and Icing, p. 10) and dunk the cone into the melts until completely coated. Do not cover the tiny hole at the bottom of the cone.

Roll the cone in a small bowl of India Tree sparkling sugar. Let it set. Lightly dust the disco dust onto the cone with a soft brush. Set the inverted cone on top of the cupcake tower.

2 To Decorate the Castle: Trace the templates of the doors, window, and flag (p. 63) onto a piece of parchment paper with a black permanent marker and cut them out. Use the templates to cut the shapes of the doors, window, and flag from the gum. Slightly dampen the gum flag with a tiny bit of water and bend to make wavy. Set aside to dry. With candy melts, glue the doors to the bottom cupcake, the window to the top cupcake, and the drageés as doorknobs.

Slice each Hi-Chew into three pieces and place around the rim of the bottom cupcake, cut side facing out, for the battlements. Press to secure.

Dust the flag with disco dust. Break the pretzel to about ¾ to 1 inch long, and glue the flag and the bead to the pretzel stick. Refrigerate to set.

Trace the template of the top battlements (p. 63) on parchment paper with a black permanent marker. Place another piece of parchment paper over it on a cookie sheet. With candy melts, trace and fill the battlements template, and refrigerate to harden. When set, place the battlements around the rim of the top cupcake, shiny side facing out, pressing to secure them.

Once the flag has set, stick the pretzel flag-pole into the tiny hole at the top of the cone, enlarging the hole if necessary.

Emeraldalicious Wand

It's so delicious, it's greenatastic!

Makes 12 wands

- 12 heart-shaped white cupcakes
- 6 cups royal icing
- AmeriColor Soft Gel Paste Food Coloring, leaf green
- AmeriColor Soft Gel Paste Food Coloring, teal green
- AmeriColor Soft Gel Paste Food Coloring, electric green
- 120 mini marshmallows

- 24 teaspoons Wilton meringue powder
- CK sanding sugar, pink
- 6 cups India Tree sparkling sugar, bright white
- 12 Sour Power candy belt, green apple
- 6 cups Wilton candy melts, green
- 12 6-inch twigs

I like to draw the leaves onto the parchment paper.

1 To Make the Heart-Shaped Cupcakes: Make ½ batch of white cupcake batter, from a boxed cake mix or homemade.

Line a 12-cup cupcake pan with liners and fill with batter as recipe directs. Crumple sheets of aluminum foil into twelve ½-inch balls and place a ball between each liner and the pan. (This indent makes a heart shape.) Bake as recipe directs. Remove to rack and let cool.

2 To Make the Emerald Heart: Tint the royal icing with the green food coloring. Use one drop at a time of each green until you have a color you like. Fill a pastry bag fitted with a #1 tip. Draw a heart shape on the cupcakes, slightly smaller than the actual cupcake. Let dry. Fill in the icing heart outline with more green icing. Push the icing to the edges of the heart with a spoon. While the icing is wet, sprinkle with sparkling sugar. Let set.

3 To Make Petals: Cut each mini marshmallow diagonally in half. Combine 2 tablespoons meringue powder and 2 tablespoons of water, mixing more as needed. Brush the mixture on the cut side of each marshmallow and dunk in pink sanding sugar. Let dry. Cut the

bottom of each marshmallow petal to make a flat side and glue around the edge of the heart with royal icing.

4 To Make Vines and Leaves: Cut each Sour Power belt into 6 long strips about ¼ to ½ inch wide. Wet the end of a strip with water, and press it onto the end of another strip, squishing the ends together, forming three vines of two strips each. Form a few small loops in the vines, wet the overlap, and press together until the loops hold. Let dry.

Prepare a Ziploc bag of the melted candy melts (Decorations, p. 11). Trace the leaves template (p. 63) on a parchment-lined cookie sheet with a black permanent marker. Place another piece of parchment paper over the tracing and trace the heart template with candy melts, making 12 to15 for each wand. Refrigerate until set.

5 To Assemble: Poke a hole in the side of the cupcake at the bottom of the heart. Insert the twig. Using the royal icing, glue the ends of the sour belt vines to the top of the twig: two vines on the left and one long vine on the right. Attach leaves to the vines with dots of green royal icing.

Pink Is Love

Send a message of love with these fun, beautiful cupcakes—perfect for all cupcake occasions, including a classroom Valentine's Day party. Spell out "Pink Is Love," someone's name, or any message you'd like.

Makes 24 cupcakes

- 24 pink cupcakes, from a boxed cake mix or homemade, pink liners
- 2 cups royal icing
- AmeriColor Soft Gel Paste Food Coloring, electric pink
- 1 piece of Twizzlers rainbow twists, pink
- 1 Trolli Peachie O's
- 1 Jelly Belly candy cane, pink/red striped
- CK sixlets, pink
- 10 candy necklace pieces, pink
- 1 Tropical Skittle, pink
- 1 Sour Power candy straw, strawberry
- candy buttons, pink
- 2 Trolli Melon O's

- 1 Sweet's saltwater taffy, pink
- 2 Sweet's jumbo gumdrop, red
- 5 Jelly Belly or Good & Plenty licorice pastels, pink
- 2 teaspoons Wilton meringue powder
- CK disco dust, rainbow
- Wilton nonpareils, white
- Wilton nonpareils, pink
- CK sanding sugar, pink
- Wilton sparkling sugar, white
- Wilton jumbo heart sprinkles, pink
- M&M's, pink
- Wilton sugar pearls, white
- CK sprinkles, pink

TO MY SWEETHEART.

1 To Ice the Cupcakes: Divide the royal icing into three bowls. Tint each with different amounts of food coloring to make three pinks: light, medium, and dark. Thin each with water, a teaspoon at a time, until the icing is about the consistency of honey. Do not add too much water, or the icing will not stay on the cupcakes. Drop a spoonful of icing onto each cupcake and spread with the back of the spoon. (It's okay if it drips down the sides a little.) Ice eight cupcakes with light pink, eight with medium pink, eight with dark pink. Let the icing set.

Prepare a Ziploc bag with royal icing (Decorations, p. 11). Set aside.

I add food coloring to the icing until I have three pinkatastic shades of pink!

2 To Make the Letters: Once the icing has set, begin spelling out "Pink Is Love," or whatever words you would like, using pieces of pink candy. Glue the candy to the cupcakes with dots of royal icing.

- Use pink rainbow Twizzlers and Peachie O's to make the letter "P."

- Use candy canes, sixlets, candy necklace pieces, Twizzlers, and Tropical Skittles to make the letters "I" and "L."

- Use Sour Power straw to make the letter "N."

- Use pink candy buttons to make the letter "K."

- Use Melon O's to make the letter "S."

- Use saltwater taffy (rolled into a snake) for the letter "V."

- Use gumdrops, rolled out in sanding sugar, and cut into a heart shape, to make the letter "O."

- Use licorice pastels for the "E."

3 To Make Other Effects: For shimmer, like the "L," "K," and "O" cupcakes, combine meringue powder and 2 tablespoons of water. With a pastry brush, paint a little meringue powder mixture on the cupcake. Sprinkle with disco dust.

For the cupcakes without letters, add white and pink nonpareils, heart sprinkles, or sanding sugar. Use royal icing to glue candy dots or white pearls in a circle, heart, or other design. For a white border, paint a bit of meringue powder around an edge and dip it into white nonpareils. Roll out gumdrop hearts and glue them in the center.

To one I love

Sweet Tooth Cupcake

Makes 12 cupcakes (each Sweet Tooth requires 2 cupcakes)

- 24 chocolate cupcakes, from a boxed cake mix or homemade, 12 in silver liners, 12 in any liner
- 12 cups buttercream frosting, store-bought or homemade, tinted with electric pink AmeriColor Soft Gel Paste Food Coloring
- Twizzlers rainbow twists
- Dubble Bubble Assorted Gumballs
- Original Skittles
- Sweet's jumbo gumdrops, assorted colors

- Haribo Raspberries gummi candy
- candy necklace
- chocolate nonpareils, rainbow
- Nitwitz Kooky Bananas
- Starzmania candy coated stars
- Jelly Bellies, assorted colors
- Jelly Belly licorice pastels, assorted colors
- peppermint starlight mints

1 Cut the tops off all 24 cupcakes so they are flat. Spread a layer of frosting, with a little height, smoothly onto the cupcakes in silver liners. Remove the liners from 12 cupcakes. They will become the top cupcakes and will rest on the frosted ones. Turn them upside down and secure to frosted cupcakes in the liners. Refrigerate until all are cool and firm.

2 Cut the square edges off the top cupcakes and carve them into domes. Spread a layer of frosting over each one. Refrigerate until set. Once set, frost all the domes generously again.

3 Wrap four tiers of different colored licorice twists around the frosting domes, starting from the bottom and going all the way around the cupcakes. Continue layering the licorice up the domes, gently pressing into the frosting to secure.

4 Prepare a Ziploc bag (or bags, if you are having a party) with the rest of the frosting (Decorations, p. 11) and carefully arrange the candy on the licorice and any exposed frosting. Pipe frosting as needed to glue the candy to the cupcakes.

Make 2 copies of the Sweet Tooth coin on p. 62 to make a paper cupcake topper. Cut out the coins and paste them together with a toothpick between them.

I'm Dreaming of a Pink Christmas

Christmas Trees

Makes 6 trees

- 6 white cupcakes, from a boxed cake mix or homemade, with silver liners
- 1 cup frosting, store-bought or homemade, white
- 2 cups frosting, store-bought or homemade, tinted with electric pink AmeriColor Soft Gel Paste Food Coloring

- 6 wafer cones
- Multicolored drageés or shimmer pearls, pink, silver, blue
- 6 Wilton jumbo star sprinkles, yellow

I love to put the cones upside down to make the Christmas tree cupcakes!

1 Spread the white frosting onto the cupcakes so there is a bit of height. Frost the wafer cones with the pink frosting, and place the cones upside down onto the frosted cupcakes.

2 Transfer half of the pink frosting into a piping bag with a #18 star tip for the first few cones. Set aside the rest for the remaining cones. Starting at the base of a cone, place the star tip on the cone, squeeze, and pull back while releasing pressure, until you get the length of spike you want, using the photograph as a guide. Pipe spikes all around the bottom of the cone, and move up, until you cover the entire cone with pink spikes.

3 Position the ornaments, evenly spaced around the trees, and place a star sprinkle atop each cupcake tree.

Snowman

The below recipe yields one chilly friend for a Pinkalicious Christmas.
To create more, just double or triple the recipe.

Makes 1 snowman

♡ 3 cake pops, one 2-inch round, one 1¾-inch round, one 1½-inch round, from a boxed cake mix or homemade (see Cake Pop Garden for cake pop instructions, p. 22)

♡ ½ cup Wilton Candy Melts, white

♡ CK sanding sugar, white

♡ 1 white cupcake, from a boxed cake mix or homemade, silver liner

♡ ½ cup frosting, store-bought or homemade, white

♡ ½ cup sweetened shredded coconut

♡ 1 Sour Power candy belt, strawberry banana

♡ 1 Smooth and Melty wafer, pink mint

♡ 1 shimmer pearl, white

♡ 2 sticks Fruit Stripe Gum, pink

♡ 1 Sweet's jumbo gumdrop, orange

♡ Wilton ready-to-use icing tube, red

♡ Wilton ready-to-use icing tube, black

♡ 3 Wonka Nerds, pink

♡ 2 pretzel sticks

1 To Make the Body: Prepare a bowl of melted candy melts (Decorations, p. 11). Place the sanding sugar in a small bowl and set aside. Using a spoon, immerse the cake balls, one at a time, in the bowl of melts until they are completely covered. Remove the balls and gently roll each ball in the sugar, coating thoroughly. Refrigerate the balls until they are set.

2 Spread the frosting onto the cupcake so there is a bit of height. Place the coconut in a small bowl and dip the frosted cupcake into the coconut, pressing the coconut into the frosting with your fingers, if necessary.

> I can spread the frosting on the cupcakes and dip them into the coconut snow.

3 Assemble Snowman: Take the cake balls out of the refrigerator and stack them together in a snowman shape, gluing each ball to the next with frosting. Using a spoon, make an indentation on the top of the cupcake and place the snowman in the indentation, pressing it gently into the coconut and frosting to secure it. Refrigerate the snowman cupcake structure briefly, until set.

To make a crown like the red one below, cut a jumbo gumdrop into a crownlike shape and roll it in white sanding sugar.

4 To Make the Crown: Cut the Sour Power belt so you have a piece with three stripes of color (yellow, pink, yellow). Snip tiny triangles from one long side of the belt to resemble the top of a crown, as in the picture. Form the belt into a circle, trimming if necessary, so that it will fit on the top of the snowman's head at a slight angle.

5 Prepare a Ziploc bag of the melts (Decorations, p. 11) and glue the circle together and the crown to the head with the melts.

6 Pipe the melts onto the top of the snowman's head, in the middle of the crown, and glue the Smooth & Melty wafer in place, topped with the shimmer pearl.

7 To Make the Scarf: Cut a stick of gum lengthwise to make two ½-inch-wide strips. Wrap one around the snowman's neck and glue it on with the melts. If the scarf does not reach completely around the neck, glue on an additional strip. Cut another strip of gum, about 1 inch long, and snip one end to make fringes. Glue the fringed piece vertically to one side of the snowman's neck, with the fringes hanging down (use this fringed piece to cover the section where the two ends of the strips come together), as on page 40.

8 To Make the Face and Buttons: Cut a small piece from the gumdrop and roll it into a cone shape for his nose. Glue it to the snowman's face with melts. Pipe the black Wilton icing onto the face for the eyes, and the

red Wilton icing for the mouth. Glue the Nerd buttons to the front of the snowman with candy melts, positioning one on the second ball and two on the third. Insert the pretzel arms at an upright angle and refrigerate the snowman briefly to set.

41

Pinkerbread House

This recipe calls for a jumbo cupcake. You'll find jumbo cupcake pans in baking specialty stores, cooking and craft stores such as Michael's and Jo-Ann's, and online. One jumbo pan typically makes 6 cupcakes, the equivalent of 12 regular-sized cupcakes.

When I make this house, my favorite part is dipping the graham cracker roof into the melts and then adding the shimmery pearls. I also love putting the gumdrops around the house for the bushes.

Makes 1 house

- ♡ 1 white jumbo cupcake, from a boxed cake mix or homemade, in a pink paper liner
- ♡ 1 cup buttercream frosting, store-bought or homemade, tinted with electric pink AmeriColor Soft Gel Paste Food Coloring
- ♡ 1 white cupcake, from a boxed cake mix or home-made
- ♡ 3 graham cracker rectangles, 2 ¼-inch by 4-inch
- ♡ ¼ cup Wilton candy melts, brown
- ♡ 20 shimmer pearls, pink
- ♡ ½ cup royal icing
- ♡ CK sanding sugar, pink
- ♡ 2 pieces of Sour Power belt candy, red
- ♡ 1 Life Saver, green

- ♡ 1 small drageé, silver
- ♡ 4 sticks Freedent spearmint gum
- ♡ 1 piece Haribo Fruity Pasta, green
- ♡ AmeriColor Soft Gel Paste Food Coloring, black
- ♡ 2 round sprinkles, yellow
- ♡ 2 jumbo nonpareils, bright pink
- ♡ 3 Sathers spice drops, 1 white, 2 green
- ♡ 1 large drageé, silver
- ♡ 1 Chiclet Tiny Size, pale pink
- ♡ 1 chocolate nonpareil, rainbow
- ♡ 2 Jujubes, green

1 Generously spread the frosting onto the jumbo cupcake so there is a bit of height. Remove the paper from the regular-sized cupcake and, with a serrated knife, cut the top of the cupcake on both sides at angles, forming the roof. Stack the smaller cupcake on top of the larger one and gently press them together. Refrigerate the cupcakes briefly to set.

2 Carefully cut one of the graham crackers into a circle. Dunk it into the melts until it is completely coated, or spread the melts on to the cracker. Let dry.

3 Once dry, spread frosting glue on the center of the cracker and set the stacked cupcakes on it. Place the structure on a cookie sheet, and place it in the refrigerator until firm.

4 When firm, gently frost the outside of the top cupcake, smoothing the frosting as much as possible. Spread some extra frosting "glue" on the angular roof of the cupcake and gently press the two graham cracker rectangles against the roof, holding them until set. Place the structure back in the refrigerator to firm up.

5 Prepare a Ziploc bag with a small amount of the buttercream frosting (Decorations, p. 11) and pipe a line of frosting where the two parts of the roof meet. While it is still soft, place the shimmer pearls on the line of frosting, pressing them gently to secure them.

6 Fill a pastry bag, fitted with a 2-inch tip, or fill a Ziploc bag with the white royal icing (Decorations, p. 11), setting aside two tablespoons. Pipe the scalloped tiles, making a crisscross pattern on both halves of the roof, as in the picture, and the edges of the roof as well. Sprinkle the sanding sugar all over the royal icing, creating a pink shimmery roof.

7 Cut a small bow out of the Sour Power candy belt. Squeeze a dot of white royal icing onto the back of the bow, and attach it to the Life Saver. Squeeze a dot or two more of icing to the back of the Life Saver and attach it to the house, on the top cupcake, right below the roof. Glue the small drageé to the center of the bow with a dot of royal icing.

8 Trace the small square window template (p. 62) onto a piece of parchment paper with a black permanent marker and cut it out. Using the template to guide you, cut a small square window out of a stick of gum and cut two rectangular shutters, the same height as the window, out of a piece of the Sour Power candy belt. Glue the window and shutters to the top cupcake with royal icing.

9 Tint the two tablespoons of reserved royal icing black, put in a Ziploc bag (Decorations, p. 11), and pipe a black cross onto the window. With the white royal icing, pipe two candles on the bottom windowpanes. Using tweezers, attach a sprinkle to the top of each candle. Secure them by pressing them gently into the royal icing.

10 Trace the two rectangular window templates (p. 62) onto a piece of parchment paper with a black permanent marker and cut them out. Cut two rectangular windows from the gum, and two small rectangular sills, the same width as the windows, out of a piece of the Sour Power candy belt. Glue the windows to the front of the bottom cupcake, leaving room to fit the door in between them. Using the black royal icing, pipe one vertical and three horizontal lines on each window. Pipe around the edge of the windows, as well. Glue a jumbo nonpareil above each window with the white royal icing. Roll out a piece of the Haribo Fruity Pasta and a white spice drop, each to ¼-inch thick. Trace the two door templates (p. 62) onto a piece of parchment paper wih a black permanent marker and cut them out. With the templates to guide you, cut out a rectangle from the Fruity Pasta that reaches from the bottom of the cupcake to the top of the windows, and a smaller rectangle from the spice drop. Glue the white rectangle on to the green rectangle with white royal icing, and glue the door on to the front of the bottom cupcake, directly between the windows.

> I pretend it's snowing when I sprinkle sugar over the roof.

11 Glue the large dragée onto the door as a handle with white royal icing. Glue the Chiclet window to the top center of the door, with white royal icing. With the black royal icing, trace the window and pipe a cross on it. Pipe three hinges on to the left side of the white part of the door.

12 Cut the chocolate nonpareil in half so that it fits above the door as an arch.

13 Cut a piece of the Sour Power candy belt for the doormat. Dip the end of the doormat, and a side of each Jujube and spice drop into the candy melts and glue them to the edge of the candy melt–coated cookie at the base of the house. Put the doormat right in front of the door, with a spice drop bush on either side and the Jujube bushes on the ends.

Pinkalicious Pinkerbelle

This pinkamazing fairy princess is made by piping icing around an inverted sugar cone,
with a yummy cake pop head and beautiful rice paper wings.

Makes 1 Pinkalicious Pinkerbelle

1 To Make the Wings:

- ♡ 1 sheet The Baker's Kitchen Edible Wafer Paper—Rice Paper
- ♡ Wilton FoodWriter, extrafine tip
- ♡ CK luster dust, orchid pink
- ♡ ¼ cup royal icing

Trace the template for Pinkalicious's wings (p. 62) onto the rice paper with edible marker and cut out the template. With your finger or a soft brush, rub luster dust onto the smooth side of the paper. Set aside.

Fill a Ziploc bag (Decorations, p. 11) or a pastry bag fitted with a #1 tip with the royal icing. Place a piece of parchment paper over the wings template on a cookie sheet. Trace the outline of the wings with royal icing. Following the template, pipe vertical lines on the wings from top to bottom, working left to right. Repeat with horizontal lines, working left to right and top to bottom over the vertical lines. Pipe dots of royal icing onto the icing grid for a lacy doily effect.

Refrigerate at least 6 hours or overnight. Once hardened, peel the parchment paper off. Glue the icing wings to the rice paper wings with a few dots of royal icing. Set aside.

2 To Make the Wand:

- ♡ 1-inch ball Wilton Gum-Tex, tinted with yellow AmeriColor Soft Gel Paste Food Coloring
- ♡ cornstarch, for dusting the work surface
- ♡ one 2 ½-inch piece of florist wire
- ♡ AmeriColor Soft Gel Paste Food Coloring, electric pink
- ♡ 2 teaspoons Wilton meringue powder
- ♡ CK disco dust, pixie dust

Knead the gum paste ball, then roll it ¼-inch thick on a work surface dusted with cornstarch. Trace the star template (p.62) onto a piece of cardboard with a black permanent marker, cut it out, and use it to cut a star from the paste.

Paint the florist wire with the electric pink food coloring, let dry, and insert into the base of the star. Let harden.

I put the Ziploc bag filled with frosting in an empty glass so it doesn't flip over and make a mess.

Combine meringue powder and 2 tablespoons of water. Using a pastry brush, brush the mixture onto the star and sprinkle with the disco dust. Set aside.

3 To Make the Head:

- ♡ one 1 ½-inch-round cake pop ball, on a 6-inch lollipop stick (see p. 22)
- ♡ ¼ cup Wilton candy melts, light pink
- ♡ ¼ cup Wilton candy melts, dark pink
- ♡ ¼ cup royal icing, tinted with electric pink Ameri-Color Soft Gel Paste Food Coloring
- ♡ 3 Wilton mini confetti sprinkles, pink

Melt the light pink candy melts (Decorations, p. 11) and immerse the cake pop ball in the bowl of melts until it is coated. Remove, let the excess drip off, and stick into a Styrofoam block to dry.

Prepare a Ziploc bag of melted dark pink candy melts (Decorations, p. 11). Trace the template for Pinkalicious's pigtails (p. 62) onto a piece of parchment paper with a black permanent marker. Place another piece over the tracing and put both on a cookie sheet. Trace and fill in the pigtails template with the candy melts. Refrigerate.

Pipe Pinkalicious's bangs onto the top of the cake pop with the candy melts. With a pastry bag fitted with a #1 tip or Ziploc bag (Decorations, p. 11), pipe royal icing for the eyebrows, eyes, nose, and mouth on the cake pop. Pipe two dots for the cheeks and attach a pink mini confetti sprinkle on each. Cut the last sprinkle in half for the ears and glue on each side with royal icing.

4 To Make the Tiara:

- 1 curved potato chip
- Linnea's luster dust, gold
- 1 teaspoon McCormick pure lemon extract
- royal icing
- CK sanding sugar, pink

With a paring knife, carve a tiara ¾-inch high from the potato chip, using the natural shape of the chip as the top and the cut side as the base of the tiara. Carve the base so it fits snugly on top of the cake pop head. Combine the gold dust with the lemon extract and paint one side of the chip gold, let dry, and paint the other.

Fill a Ziploc bag with royal icing (Decorations, p. 11) and pipe seven dots of royal icing along the front top edge of the chip. Sprinkle the dots with pink sanding sugar.

> I choose the potato chip we use to make the crown. Then I try not to eat the rest.

5 To Make the Body and Skirt:

- 1 sugar cone
- Pink cupcake, from a boxed cake mix or homemade
- 2 cups buttercream frosting, store-bought or homemade, tinted light pink with a drop or two of electric pink AmeriColor Soft Gel Paste Food Coloring
- 1 Jelly Belly licorice pastel, pink
- ½ cup frosting, store-bought or homemade, tinted dark pink with several drops of electric pink AmeriColor Soft Gel Paste Food Coloring
- 1 Laffy Taffy, pink
- 1 piece of Sour Power candy belt, red
- 2 Pocky sticks, strawberry
- ¼ cup royal icing

Trim ½ to ¾ inch off the pointy tip of the sugar cone, making a hole large enough for the cake pop stick. Set the cupcake upside down on a doily-lined cake circle. Shave the top edges of cupcake into a slight cone shape so it fits inside the upside-down sugar cone. The cupcake should stick out ½ an inch around the bottom of the cone. Spread light pink frosting under the cupcake/cone to glue it to the cake circle. Starting from the top, spread a generous layer of the light pink frosting about a quarter of the way down the cupcake/cone. This will be the shirt. Build it up to a cylinder shape with more frosting.

Spread additional frosting all around the bottom to make the skirt flare. Gradually smooth the frosting up the cone, stopping at the bottom of the shirt. Spread an additional 1 inch of frosting all the way around the base of the cone. Refrigerate until hardened.

Fill a pastry bag fitted with a coupler and a #104 tip with light pink buttercream frosting. Place the cupcake/cone body on a cake turntable. If you do not have a turntable, you will need to spin the cake circle with one hand as you pipe the pleats of the dress with your other.

Starting ¼ inch below the bottom of the shirt, hold the pastry bag at a 45-degree angle so that the hole of the tip rests against the dress. As you slowly spin the turntable with one hand, squeeze the pastry bag with the other, gently pull the tip away from the dress, and bring it back to the dress repeatedly, moving around the skirt and forming one continuous row of three-dimensional ruffles. Leaving ¼ inch between tiers, start the second tier of frosting ruffles and continue piping tiers until ¼ inch from the bottom of the skirt.

Unscrew the coupler, remove the #104 tip, and replace with a star #27 tip. Pipe a line of stars around the very top of the skirt, the very bottom of the skirt, and in between each tier, filling in the ¼-inch gaps.

Cut the licorice pastel in half for shoes and stick them into the frosting, 2 inches apart, at the bottom of the skirt.

Fill a clean pastry bag, fitted with a coupler and star 27 tip with the dark pink frosting, and pipe stars all over the shirt, building the shoulders and sleeves. Leave the hole at the top of the cone uncovered.

Roll a small piece of the taffy into a ½-inch diameter donut shape for the neck. Make the hole of the donut match the size of the hole at the top of the cone. Glue the donut neck on top of the hole with a bit of the dark pink frosting. Refrigerate until hardened.

Cut a tiny ribbon shape out of the Sour Power candy belt.

Once hardened, remove the project from the refrigerator, cut off 1 ½ inches from the top of each Pocky stick and in-sert the cut end of each one into a frosting sleeve for arms.

Fill a Ziploc bag with the royal icing (Decorations, p. 11) and pipe a thin line around the bottom of each sleeve and the neckline of the shirt. Glue the sour belt ribbon to the middle of the neckline with royal icing.

6 Assembly

♡ **¼ cup Wilton candy melts, dark pink**

Prepare a Ziploc bag of melted dark pink candy melts (Decorations, p. 11).

Carefully insert the cake pop stick straight into the hole at the end of the cone and push down through the cup-cake, until the head rests on top of the cone.

Remove pigtails from the refrigerator and make a cut on each side of the head above ears. Pipe candy melts into each cut, peel the candy melt pigtails off the paper, and insert a pigtail into each side of the head.

Pipe a line of candy melts at the top for the bangs and glue the tiara on. Squeeze more candy melts behind it to secure it and keep it upright.

Position one wing behind the body so that the bottom of the wing hits the bottom of the first tier of skirt pleats. If needed, carve the back and remove some frosting so that the wings can stand straight. Squeeze candy melts onto the inner edge of the wing, glue it to the body, and hold in place for a few seconds until candy melts harden. Pipe additional candy melts on top of the wing joint. Repeat for the other wing.

Insert the end of the star wand into the second tier of frosting in front of the right hand.

Pinkalicious's Family and Friends

Let's make cupcakes that look like some favorite PINKALICIOUS characters. There's Mommy and Daddy and Peter, Mr. Swizzle the ice cream man, Pinkalicious's teacher Mr. Pushkin, and even some of Pinkalicious's classmates. You can use candy and frosting to make faces that look like your family, friends, and neighbors, too!

Family and Friends Basic Preparation

♡ White cupcake, from a boxed cake mix or homemade (p. 6)
♡ ½ cup frosting, store-bought or homemade, for each cupcake, tinted with copper fleshtone AmeriColor Soft Gel Paste Food Coloring

Cut off the tops of the cupcakes if needed to make a flat surface, and cover smoothly with the tinted frosting.
Prepare as many cupcakes as you need, but because faces can be tricky, it's a good idea to prepare a few extra.

Mommy

♡ ¼ cup brown Wilton candy melts
♡ ¼ cup white Wilton candy melts
♡ 2 Wilton jumbo rainbow nonpareils, dark blue
♡ 1 Tootsie Roll

♡ 1 Starburst, pink
♡ Wilton sparkling sugar, white
♡ 1 Sweet's jumbo gumdrop, red
♡ Wilton ready-to-use icing tube, red

1 To Make the Hair: Prepare a bowl of melted white candy melts (Decorations, p. 11) and set aside.

2 Squeeze a few brown melts into the bowl of white melts and stir with a wooden spoon to create a light brown color. Prepare a Ziploc bag of this.

3 Trace the template (p. 62) for Mommy's hair onto a piece of parchment paper with a black permanent marker. Place another piece of parchment paper over the tracing and put both on a cookie sheet. Using the bag of brown candy melts, trace the template for the hair. (You'll be able to see it through the parchment paper.) Fill in the template with the brown candy melts. Refrigerate the sheet until the hair has hardened.

4 Remove the candy-melt hair from the refrigerator and carefully peel it off the parchment paper with an offset spatula. Place the hair on a frosted cupcake.

5 To Make the Face: With tweezers, place the two nonpareil sprinkles for the eyes. Make two very thin, short Tootsie Roll strings and one slightly longer one. Place the two shorter strings for the eyebrows and use the longer string for the nose.

6 On a nonstick surface sprinkled with white sparkling sugar, roll out the Starburst and jumbo gumdrop to ⅛ inch. Cut out two small discs from the Starburst for the cheeks and a moon shape from the gumdrop for the mouth. Place on the cupcake. Pipe the decorating icing on to the mouth, covering it. With tweezers, gently press all of the candy features into the frosting to secure them.

Daddy

- ♡ a handful of chocolate vermicelli sprinkles
- ♡ 1 tablespoon frosting, store bought or homemade, tinted with chocolate brown AmeriColor Soft Gel Paste Food Coloring
- ♡ 1 Wilton jumbo confetti sprinkle, orange
- ♡ 2 regular-sized chocolate sprinkles
- ♡ 1 Tootsie Roll
- ♡ 1 Starburst, pink strawberry
- ♡ 1 Sour Power candy belt, red

1 To Make the Hair: Place the vermicelli sprinkles in a small bowl and set aside. Prepare a Ziploc bag with the chocolate-brown frosting (Decorations, p. 11) and set aside.

2 Trace Daddy's hair template (p. 62) onto a piece of parchment paper with a black permanent marker and cut it out. Gently place Daddy's hair template on a frosted cupcake and pipe the chocolate-brown frosting around the edge of the template. Remove the template and fill in the hair. Carefully dunk the frosting hair into the sprinkles.

3 To Make the Face: Score and cut the confetti sprinkle and position it upright for the ear. Stick the two regular-sized sprinkles vertically, like pins, into the frosting for the eyes. Make two very thin, short Tootsie Roll strings and one slightly longer one. Place the two shorter strings for the eyebrows and use the longer string for the nose.

4 Roll out the Starburst to ⅛-inch thick on a nonstick surface. Cut out a small disc for the cheek from the Starburst and cut a moon shape for the mouth from the Sour Belt. Position the cheek and mouth on the cupcake.

Peter

- ♥ 1 Taffy Town saltwater taffy, grape
- ♥ 1 Tootsie Roll
- ♥ ¼ cup white Wilton Candy Melts
- ♥ 2 Wilton jumbo rainbow nonpareils, dark blue
- ♥ 1 Wilton jumbo confetti sprinkle, orange
- ♥ 1 Starburst, pink strawberry
- ♥ 1 AirHeads taffy, red

1 To Make the Hat: Roll out the Taffy Town taffy to ⅛ inch thick on a nonstick surface. Cut out the semicircular shape of the hat, making sure it is wide enough to cover one-third of the cupcake. Cut out a finger-shaped piece for the hat's brim.

2 Make very thin, short Tootsie Roll strings for the hair, the nose, and the eyebrows. Set aside the nose and eyebrow pieces. Using the hat as a guide but not securing it quite yet, place several pieces of the Tootsie Roll hair vertically in a line on the right side of the cupcake and a few pieces on the left side. Position the hat on the top of the cupcake, so that the hair is sticking out from under it on either side.

3 Prepare a Ziploc bag of the melted candy melts (Decorations, p. 11) and set it aside.

4 Insert a toothpick horizontally into the left side of the cupcake where the brim of the hat will be, leaving ½ inch of the toothpick sticking out as a support for the brim. Pipe some candy melts on the toothpick and attach the brim to the toothpick. Pipe additional melts where necessary to ensure the brim is attached to the hat and that the hat is attached to the cupcake.

5 To Make the Face: With tweezers, place the two nonpareil sprinkles on the cupcake for the eyes. Score and cut out the confetti sprinkle and position it upright for the ear. Position the reserved pieces of the Tootsie Roll string on to the cupcake for the eyebrows and nose.

6 Roll out the Starburst to ⅛-inch thick on a nonstick surface. Cut a small circle and a half circle with a rounded edge from the Starburst. Position the circle piece for the cheek and position the half-circle on the left side of the cupcake for the other cheek. Cut a small, thin moon shape from the AirHeads taffy and position it for the mouth at a crooked angle.

Mr. Pushkin

- ♡ 2 pieces of Twizzlers chocolate twists
- ♡ 1 Tootsie Roll
- ♡ 1 Jelly Belly licorice pastel, black
- ♡ 2 Wilton jumbo confetti sprinkles, orange
- ♡ 1 Jelly Belly, pink
- ♡ 1 Wilton mini confetti sprinkle, orange
- ♡ 1 Wilton jumbo confetti sprinkle, blue

1 To Make the Hair: Cut the chocolate licorice lengthwise into 1/8-inch strips. Trim the strips into varying lengths, 1 to 2 inches long, and cut one end of each strip into a point. Arrange the strips on the cupcake, pointed ends facing down, in the shape of hair, trimming as necessary to create the hairline.

2 To Make the Face: Make two very thin, short Tootsie Roll strings for one eyebrow and the nose, and two tiny balls for the eyes. Place the eyes, then place the eyebrow and nose.

3 On a nonstick surface, roll out the Jelly Belly licorice pastel to 1/8-inch thick. Cut a small, thin moon shape and position it for the mouth.

5 Carefully slice off a sliver of one of the orange jumbo confetti sprinkles, leaving a slight curve. Position it so that the sprinkle fits snugly at the edge of the right side of the cupcake. Position the whole orange jumbo confetti sprinkle for the left cheek. Cut the pink Jelly Belly in half and position it for the left ear.

6 To Make the Bow Tie: Place the mini confetti sprinkle on the middle of the bottom edge of the cupcake. Cut the blue jumbo confetti sprinkle in half for the two collar pieces and put half on either side of the mini sprinkle with the cut sides resting on the edge of the cupcake and the curved sides facing down and off the cupcake.

To make sure the candies don't fall off, I gently press them into the cupcake when everything is in the right place.

Sophia

- ♡ ¼ cup Wilton candy melts, brown
- ♡ 1 Bassett's Liquorice Allsorts, black
- ♡ 2 teaspoons Wilton meringue powder
- ♡ 1 tablespoon rainbow sparkling sugar
- ♡ 1 piece Gustaf's strawberry laces
- ♡ 1 blue sprinkle
- ♡ Wilton sparkling sugar, white
- ♡ 1 Sweet's jumbo gumdrop, red

1 To Make the Hair: Prepare a Ziploc bag of the melted candy melts (Decorations, p. 11) and set it aside.

2 Trace Sophia's hair template (p. 62) onto a parchment-lined cookie sheet with a black permanent marker. Place another piece of parchment paper over the tracing (you'll be able to see it through the paper) and using the candy melts, trace Sophia's hair template. Fill in the template with the brown candy melts. Refrigerate until the hair has hardened.

3 Remove the hair from the refrigerator and carefully peel it off the parchment paper with an offset spatula. Place the hair on top of the frosted cupcake.

4 To Make the Glasses: Slice a Bassett's Liquorice Allsorts in half. Combine the meringue powder and 2 tablespoons of water. Using a pastry brush, brush a little of the meringue powder mixture onto the cut sides of the Allsorts. Place the rainbow sparkling sugar in a small bowl and dunk the Allsorts into the sugar. Position the Allsorts, sparkling sugar sides up, where the eyes go. Gently press them into the frosting with tweezers or a knife, not fingers.

5 Complete the glasses by cutting three short ⅛- to ¼-inch pieces of licorice lace. Place one piece of licorice lace in between the sparkling sugar–covered Allsorts for the bridge of Sophia's glasses. Place two more pieces of lace on either side of the Allsorts for the arms of the glasses.

6 To Make the Nose: Put the blue sprinkle onto the cupcake at a slant.

7 To Make the Mouth: On a nonstick surface sprinkled with white sparkling sugar, roll out the jumbo gumdrop to ⅛-inch thick. Cut out a small oval. Position it at a slight angle.

Pauline

- 2 pieces of Twizzlers rainbow twists, orange, yellow
- 1 piece of Twizzlers chocolate twist
- 1 Tootsie Roll
- 2 Wilton jumbo rainbow nonpareils, black
- 1 Starburst, pink
- Twizzlers licorice twist, black
- 1 Necco Wafer, brown
- AmeriColor Gourmet Writer, black
- 1 Wilton mini confetti sprinkle, blue
- 1 tablespoon royal icing

1 To Make the Hair: Cut the orange, yellow, and chocolate Twizzlers lengthwise into ⅛-inch strips. Trim the strips into varying lengths, ¼- to 1-inch long, and cut one end of each strip into a point. Arrange the strips in the shape of her hair on the top edge of the cupcake with the pointed ends facing down. Add longer strips on the left and right edges.

2 To Make the Face: Make three very thin Tootsie Roll strings and place them on the cupcake for the eyebrows and nose.

3 To Make the Eyes: Put the two nonpareil sprinkles on the cupcake.

4 To Make the Mouth: Cut a circle out of the black licorice and position on the cupcake.

5 To Make the Cheek: Roll out the Starburst to ⅛-inch thick and cut out two small discs for the cheeks.

6 To Make the Collar: Gently cut the Necco wafer in half. With the edible marker, draw squiggles on the Necco Wafer halves to make a leopard print. Position the Necco Wafer halves on the bottom of the cupcake with the cut sides resting on the bottom edge and the curved sides facing down and off the cupcake.

7 Fill a Ziploc bag with the royal icing (Decorations, p. 11) and squeeze a dot of royal icing in the middle of where the two Necco wafers meet. Place the mini confetti sprinkle on the royal icing dot.

Brittany

- 1 piece of Twizzlers chocolate twist
- 1 piece of Twizzlers strawberry twist
- 3 pieces of Twizzlers rainbow twists, orange, yellow, light red
- ¼ cup royal icing
- 2 Wilton jumbo rainbow nonpareils, black
- 1 Tootsie Roll
- 1 piece of Twizzlers licorice twist, black
- 1 Starburst, pink

1 To Make the Hair: Cut the chocolate, strawberry, orange, yellow, and light red Twizzlers into ⅛-inch strips. Trim the strips into varying lengths, ¼- to 1-inch long, and cut one end of each strip into a point. Arrange the different-colored strips in an arc on the top edge of the cupcake with the pointed ends facing down to form her bangs. Add a few longer strips on the left and right edges, to form the sides of her hair. Trim the tops of the strips to match the round curve of the cupcake.

2 Poke a small hole into the side of the cupcake, above and in the middle of the bangs, where the ponytail will come out. Fill a Ziploc bag with the royal icing (Decorations, p. 11) and squeeze the icing into the hole. Insert the longer strips of Twizzlers hair so that they poke out at different lengths.

3 To Make the Face: Place the two nonpareils on the cupcake for the eyes.

4 Make three very thin Tootsie Roll strings for the eyebrows and nose. Place the three pieces of the Tootsie Roll string on the cupcake.

5 Cut a teardrop shape out of the black licorice and position it on the cupcake under the nose at a diagonal so that the pointed end is on the top right.

6 Roll out the Starburst to ⅛-inch thick on a nonstick surface. Cut out two small discs. Place them for the cheeks.

Mr. Swizzle

♡ ¼ cup Wilton candy melts, brown
♡ 2 Wilton jumbo rainbow nonpareils, dark blue
♡ 1 Starburst, pink
♡ 1 Tootsie Roll
♡ 1 candy necklace, pink piece
♡ 1 Sour Power candy belt, red

♡ 1 large marshmallow
♡ 1 Chiclet Tiny Size, maroon
♡ Wilton Sprinkles, sparkling sugar, white
♡ 1 Sweet's jumbo gumdrop, red
♡ Wilton ready-to-use icing tube, red

1 To Make the Hair: Prepare a Ziploc bag of the melted candy melts (Decorations, p. 11) and pipe the candy melts onto the top edge of the cupcake for the hair.

2 To Make the Face: Place the two jumbo nonpareils on the cupcake for the eyes.

3 Roll out the Starburst to ⅛-inch thick on a nonstick surface. Cut out two small discs. Place them for the cheeks.

4 Make three very thin, short Tootsie Roll strings and place them on the cupcake for the eyebrows and nose.

5 With the candy melts, pipe the moustache onto the cupcake, beginning under the nose and curling each end into a swirl on top of the cheeks.

6 Cut the candy necklace piece in half and position the two halves on each side of the cupcake for ears.

7 On a nonstick surface sprinkled with sparkling sugar, roll out the jumbo gumdrop to ⅛-inch thick. Cut out a moon shape for the mouth and place the mouth on the cupcake. Pipe the decorating icing onto the mouth, covering it with icing.

8 To Make the Bow Tie: Cut a bow-tie shape out of the Sour Power belt. Place the bow tie at the bottom edge of the cupcake in the center. With the decorating icing, outline the bow tie in red. Squeeze a tiny dot of decorating icing in the middle of the bow tie, and attach the Chiclet so that it lies on the bow horizontally.

9 To Make the Hat: Cut the marshmallow in half crosswise. Stick the marshmallow, cut side down, on top of the candy melts hair in the center, using extra candy melts to secure it.

10 With the decorating icing, pipe thin red trim around the top edge of the marshmallow.

Cupcake Palette

What is your favorite color? Pink? Purple? Green? Blue? Whatever it is, these easy-to-make colorlicious treats are a feast for the eyes. Add to the fun with a cookie paintbrush. Three guesses what the bristles are . . . give up? Chewing gum!

Makes 24 cupcakes and 6 cookie paintbrushes

1 To Make the Cupcakes:

- ♡ 1 batch of white cupcake batter, from a boxed cake mix or homemade
- ♡ White icing, store-bought or homemade
- ♡ AmeriColor Soft Gel Paste Food Coloring, electric pink, electric blue, electric purple, electric green, electric yellow, electric orange

Divide the batter into 6 small bowls. Squeeze a few drops of a different color into each bowl of batter and whisk, then bake following manufacturer's or Basics (p. 4) instructions. Use four 6-cup baking tins, as in the photo, or use two 12-cup tins.

> **For filled cupcakes, use an injector tip or cut a small cone shape out of the top of the baked cupcake, fill with white icing, and replace the cone shape.**

2 To Make the Brushes:

- ♡ ½ of a 16.5-ounce package of ready-to-bake sugar cookie dough
- ♡ ¼ cup all-purpose flour, plus more for dusting the work surface
- ♡ ½ cup Wilton candy melts, white
- ♡ 24 sticks Freedent spearmint gum
- ♡ 1 tablespoon McCormick pure lemon extract
- ♡ Gold Gourmet edible silver leaf dust

Preheat oven to 350° and line two cookie sheets with parchment paper.

In a medium bowl, combine cookie dough with flour, kneading flour completely into the dough. Roll out on a nonstick surface dusted with flour. Divide into 6 pieces and roll each into a 6-inch-long by ½-inch-thick rope with slightly tapered ends.

Bake for 10 to 12 minutes, rotating pans halfway through. Cookies are done when very firm and brown around the edges. Transfer to a wire rack and cool to room temperature.

Prepare a Ziploc bag of the melted candy melts (Decorations, p, 11).

Trim a stick of gum to wrap snugly, without overlap, around one end of a cookie. Gum should extend ¼ inch over the tip of the cookie. With candy melts, glue the gum to the end of cookie. Repeat with second stick of gum.

Fold the third and fourth sticks of gum in half crosswise, one at a time. Slice the unfolded end of the gum to make a head of bristles. Do not cut all the way to the folded end. Gently press the bottom parts together, forming one head with many bristles.

With candy melts, glue the bristle bundle to the end of the cookie wrapped in gum.

Combine lemon extract and silver dust and paint the gum wrapped around the cookie a rich silver metallic color. Repeat with the remaining 5 paintbrushes.

Mix a few drops of electric pink coloring into the icing to make dark pink. Decorate the tips of the cookie bristles with it.

Templates

All templates are actual size

Family and Friends
pp. 52–59

Mommy's hair

Daddy's hair

Sophia's hair

Sweet Tooth Cupcake
p. 36

Sweet Tooth coin

Pinkerbread House
pp. 42–45

upper window

lower windows

door

door

Pinkalicious Pinkerbelle
pp. 46–49

wing

star wand

Pinkalicious's pigtails

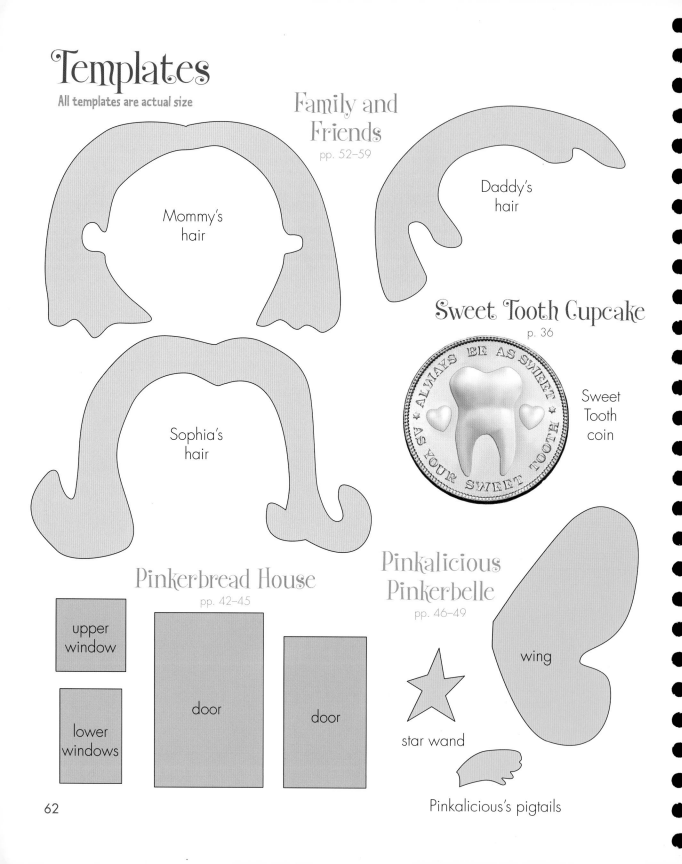

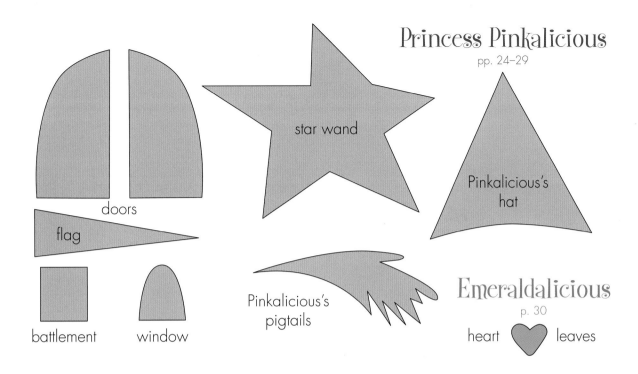

doors

flag

battlement

window

Princess Pinkalicious
pp. 24–29

star wand

Pinkalicious's hat

Pinkalicious's pigtails

Emeraldalicious
p. 30

heart   leaves

Metric Equivalents

Fahrenheit/Celsius/Gas Mark Equivalents

- 275°F = 140°C = gas mark 1
- 300°F = 150°C = gas mark 2
- 325°F = 165°C = gas mark 3
- 350°F = 180°C = gas mark 4
- 375°F = 190°C = gas mark 5
- 400°F = 200°C = gas mark 6

Length equivalents

- ¼ inch = .5 cm
- ½ inch = 1 cm
- 1 inch = 2.5 cm
- 6 inches = 15 cm
- 1 foot (12 inches) = 30 cm

Weight Equivalents

- ½ ounce = 15 grams (rounded; exact = 14)
- 1 ounce = 30 grams (exact 28)
- 2 ounces = 55 grams (exact 56)
- 4 ounces = ¼ pound = 115 grams (exact 113)
- 8 ounces = ½ pound = 225 grams (exact 227)
- 12 ounces = ¾ pound = 340 grams (exact)
- 16 ounces = 1 pound = 455 grams (exact 454)

Sources

Cake decorating and baking supplies such as pastry bags and tips, food coloring, cupcake pans and liners, and gluten-free mixes, as well as all kinds of candies, edible decorations, edible rice paper, and edible ink markers are available online. Below are several good sources, but be sure to check your local grocery and hobby stores as well.

Bob's Red Mill (gluten-free mixes and general baking ingredients)
www.bobsredmill.com

Candy Warehouse (candy)
www.candywarehouse.com

CandiWorks (candy)
(no website)
353 Canal St
New York, NY 10013

Confectionery House (specialty baking pans, specialty cake decorating supplies including glitter, sanding sugar, sixlets, dragees, edible pearls, etc.)
www.confectioneryhouse.com

Economy Candy (candy)
www.economycandy.com
108 Rivington Street
New York, NY 10012

Fuzziwigs Candy Factory stores (candy)
www.fuzziwigscandyfactory.com

Hobby Lobby (baking pans and cake decorating supplies)
www.hobbylobby.com

King Arthur (gluten-free mixes and cake decorating supplies)
www.kingarthurflour.com

Jo-Ann (baking pans and liners, cake decorating supplies)
www.joann.com/baking

Michaels (baking pans and liners, cake decorating supplies)
www.michaels.com

N.Y. Cake (specialty baking pans, specialty cake decorating supplies including luster dust, glitter, sanding sugar, sixlets, dragees, edible pearls, food coloring, etc.)
www.nycake.com

Pfeil & Holing (for professional decorators: specialty baking pans, specialty cake decorating supplies including luster dust, disco dust, food coloring)
www.cakedeco.com

sur la table (baking pans and liners, cake decorating supplies)
www.surlatable.com

Madame Alexander doll on page 13
www.madamealexander.com

Pinkalicious cupcake wraps and edible images (not shown)
www.decopac.com

Pinkalicious party supplies (not shown)
www.favors.com